Reflections in Running Water

—Collected Poetry—

By Thomas Pietrosanti

First paperback edition October, 2023

Cover photography and design by Thomas Pietrosanti

ISBN 979-8-9882523-0-6 (paperback)
ISBN 979-8-9882523-1-3 (ebook)

Published by Thomas Pietrosanti
pietrosanti.publishing@gmail.com

Contents

Give and Take

Demons, Quests, and Pests

To Sleep, To Dream, To Write

NATURAL RHYTHMS

I HEAR THE OCEAN SCRAPE THE CLOUDS

I hear the ocean scrape the clouds
And wait for their reply.
I watch the pain come falling down
As anger splits the sky.

A darkness hides what once was clear
And steals the warmth away.
No stars above by which to steer,
The lost are led astray.

Two halves of one infinity
Find standing in their eye,
A sparkle of divinity
Whose essence they decry.

But as the spark consumes the wind
Its glow intensifies.
And in the light of truth, chagrined,
Those gods of seas and skies.

Upon an iridescent lawn,
Which from the sky was hewn,
It glitters idly in the dawn
Reflected from the moon.

THE SHAPE OF WATER

No matter in what it is held
To that shape will water meld
But when it rests all on its own
Only then is water known

BRUSH AND BERRY

Crashing through the brush and berry,
Chasing prancing tines.
Ever were our hearts so merry
There beneath the pines.

Splashing barefoot in the creekbed,
Turning every stone.
Hunting with a wooden spearhead
While the sun yet shone.

Climbing high as we were dared to,
Up a lofty perch.
Not admitting we were scared to
Bend a youthful birch.

Rhyming lines we'd be ashamed by
Were they overheard.
Recklessness, as such, was tamed by
Shouting out a word.

Though our boots tread separate trails, we
Keep our hearts as one.
Souls eternal dance the valley
Under setting sun.

SUN AND RAIN
Sweet summer smells, milk-butter swells
As bee returns to flower.
Cock early crows, the farmer knows:
Mid-morning it will shower.

He lifts his head up from the bed
To take a look around.
No time to wait or hesitate,
His feet are on the ground.

Without a thought as he'd been taught,
On instinct he reacts.
But coming rain relieves the strain,
Today he can relax.

The seeds are sewn, though not much grown,
God's work has just begun.
The cooling mist is to assist
The warming of the sun.

When skies are grey there's time to play,
No chores hang overhead.
A bluer sky makes spirits high,
But work is done instead.

Ironically this balance be
Required to survive,
But till the earth with joy and mirth
And watch your garden thrive.

PLANTING SEEDS AND PULLING WEEDS

All day in the sun and soil,
Knowing only sweat and toil,
With a gentle calloused hand
I have worked and tilled the land.

Children join me in the field,
Helping to increase our yield.
Watching all that I have nourished
As they rooted, grew, and flourished.

Then we rest beneath the trees,
Lulled by humming honeybees,
'til we sow the fruits of labors
'mongst our family, friends, and neighbors.

Musing as the sunlight wanes,
And sets aflame the rolling plains,
That I have done no finer deeds
Than planting seeds and pulling weeds.

NEW ENGLAND POTATOES

Our greatest crop arrives in May
(Not tobacco, corn, or hay).
We harvest as we plow our fields,
Always shocked by ample yields.

Every year our bounty grows,
Which we transplant in tidy rows
To where our neighbors all agree
We separate our property.

THE HUNTER'S LULLABY

I set myself at ease beneath
My favorite hunting tree.
Across my lap carefully lies
My chosen weaponry.

The sun had yet to climb atop
Yon eastward peaks of birch,
When from above descended dove
Whom on my hat did perch.

"Does he not know that I am foe?"
I asked to none by me.
That bird, he heard, and then replied
By chirping merrily.

When all at once from over hill
There came a mighty breath.
The trees around me then began
To whisper songs of death.

The chill ran up and down my back
But shivered not my bones.
Unlike my face, my heart was warmed
By dove's melodic tones.

Though shadows short, I stretched my jaw—
It was the song that lulled.
Then I, the hunter, proud and strong,
From hunt to dreams was culled.

While in my dreams there came a stag
Who stood before my gun.
With nothing but a gentle squeeze
I'd have my trophy won.

But something stayed my trembling hand
And calmed my ragged breath.
I could not interrupt the flute
Of life with horns of death.

Instead I voyaged through the lands
Untouched by hands of men.
Where if some day I get the chance,
I'd like to go again.

The dove continued singing, though
His song fell on deaf ears.
The duet played of flute and horn
Is not what it appears.

Now if you travel to that spot
And look beneath that tree,
A monument to nature's might,
A statue you will see.

BLOSSOM

The thoughts have been thought,
The words have been spoken.
Their senses are taut,
Their spirits awoken.

The river's aswell,
The stream water quickens.
Replacing what fell,
The young sapling thickens.

When warm became cold,
Their tears became frozen.
The young became old,
The choosing now chosen.

A delicate breath,
So warm and inviting,
Arouses from death
A spark reigniting.

A twist and a curve,
Their roots intertwining.
A sway and a swerve,
Their bodies aligning.

Stretched up to the sky,
Her petals spread wider.
She must satisfy
The urges inside her.

For nectar they come,
All dancing and drinking
And beating a drum
Til daylight is shrinking.

Spread out on the floor
Lie petals discarded.
They visit no more,
Those guests now departed.

The flower's sweet smell,
No longer detected.
Beginning to swell,
A change is expected.

Drawn up from the root,
The spirits endow her
With ripening fruit
And ancestor's power.

The flowers they mourn
Have finished preparing.
This burden they've born,
The branches now bearing

Til one day they're grown,
No longer protected,
Each taken and sewn
By those who collected.

Though rooted in place,
By distance divided,
Through spirit and grace,
Forever united.

NEW GROWTH IN OLD WOODS

An ancient forest, proud and tall,
On top of which the flyers call,
Its roots are deep, its branches wide,
The Sun from Earth their shadows hide.

Beneath the treetops in the dark
Stand sturdy columns swathed in bark.
The emerald mural they uphold
Has recently been lined with gold.

But with myself alone I share
These regal halls so vast and bare.
A rusty carpet of the dead
Across the empty floor is spread.

Like tired leaves are shed the seeds,
Who briefly dance along the breeze
Before they rest on forest floor,
Upon which they would dance no more.

The lucky few who get to sprout—
And are not promptly weeded out—
Will have to fight for any share
Of which the ancients deign to spare.

The handful, then, that do survive
Are able to in darkness thrive,
And one must ask if it is right
For plants to grow without the light.

This generation, green and new,
Despite the fact that they be few,
It will be they who must stand tall
And watch the leaves of fathers fall.

THE AUTUMN WIND

Be to me the autumn wind
With scent of smoke and cinnamon.
Soothe the burning of my skin
And rescue me from temptation.

Be the dawning crest of sun
Whose waning light has just begun.
Gently kiss my frosted cheek
To make me strong and leave me weak.

Bring to me a gift of gold
As in the ancient stories told.
Hold me tight against your breast
Then squeeze until I've decompressed.

Wake me when the light returns,
But not until its brightness burns,
For only through its righteous pain
Can I be sure I live again.

WATCH IT BURN

I sit and watch the forest burn
With little heed and no concern.
The colors keep me in a trance
While they flicker, sway, and dance.

I watch as embers fly and fall
And hear the raven's warning call,
And yet unmoved I sit and stare
While breathing in the smoky air.

Once the flames have all consumed,
The forest—being amply groomed—
No longer holds me in a thrall
And frees me from the siren's call.

Some find it supernatural,
Yet others simply rational.
To me, it is a work of art
Which frees the mind and snares the heart.

THE LAST BREATH OF AUTUMN

As the heat of passion's kiss
Fades into lovers' bliss,
And a soft and gentle sigh
Ascends the burning sky.

Mem'ry forms upon the lips
Of gentle fingertips,
Whispered through the tangled limbs
As skyward lantern dims.

In the darkness which ensues,
Now framed by violet hues,
Glisten pairs of sightless eyes
Reflecting empty skies.

Candles carried into night
Will cast a trembling light.
Shadows' dance distracts from frost—
A beacon to the lost.

Flames are fallen, bones arise,
Outstretched to southern skies.
Grasping for that distant heat,
Denying their defeat.

For as yet there does reside
(Though hidden deep inside),
Memory which can revive,
And by its warmth survive.

LOSING THE LIGHT

From the river's rocky berth
I watch my love depart,
Falling off the edge of Earth
And dragging down my heart.

Southwards migrate summer birds
Who flee the coming chills,
Carrying the springtime words
And dropping empty quills.

With them, dark and icy lines
I scratch into the page,
Frozen like the winter pines
Upon a gleaming stage.

A letting of the poisoned blood—
A crude, archaic cure.
Cleansing with a purging flood
Whose heir is fresh and pure.

By shore the lake and land defined,
Their essence but ignored.
Yet we are soul and skin combined,
By both our worth is scored.

And so it is that I proclaim
And harvest all the blame.
Before the sky is lit aflame,
I must forsake my name.

Then like a phoenix in that flame,
My heart shall be reborn.
And hence the shadow of my shame
Shall wither in her scorn.

A WAKE OF FROST

The sun is warm,
The wind is cold.
The day is young,
The season old.

The vine has withered,
Growing mold.
The kings are wrapped
In cloaks of gold.

A feast is shared
'mongst fam'ly, friends.
Ere in a hush
The vale descends.

As spirits lifted
From the ground
Are freed from whence
They had been bound.

Upon their trail
A wake of frost—
A memory
Of what was lost.

SCARRED

Untouched fields of crystal dew,
Painted in a morning hue,
Soften Gaia's aging lines—
Mask her scars and blunt her spines.

Paths are covered and effaced,
Hist'ry—for a time—erased.
Ways of future ancestors
Etched now for their followers.

Quickly is the canvas filled—
Ink upon the parchment spilled.
This, too, will evaporate—
Body will regenerate.

Memoirs etched upon her flesh—
Consequence of mankind's thresh—
Patterns one may only spy
Looking through celestial eye.

A DYING SKY

The old sky ignites
In a flare of defiance,
Refusing concession
To laws known by science.

The furious crimson
Of fast-dying light
Paints canvas of blue
To the viewers' delight.

The red against blue
Yields a violet hue;
The colors unite
And then fade into night.

TO DAY REBORN

The sun has dimmed
The winds have stilled
The day is dying
The trees agild

The sky is dark
The air is bitter
The light has died
The branches glitter

Throughout the chill
Of endless night
When all is wrapped
In sheets of white

By following
A modest light
The lost are guided
Through their plight

The sun will rise
The winds will shout
To day reborn
New forests sprout

BIRDSONG

The air is filled with bawdy song—
The sounds of Springtime lust—
Awakening the nighttime long
And shaking off the dust.

The thawing chill that frosts the morn
And captures words in flight
Evaporates as sun is borne,
Returning in the night.

From icy claws, we hide away
Within protective shell
Until that long-awaited day
When hearts our minds must quell.

The time has come to make a leap
Into the open sky.
Farewell to safety, warmth, and sleep;
It's time to learn to fly.

LAWS OF ATTRACTION

OPPOSITES COLLIDE

We passed each other
On opposite paths,
You heading north
While I travelled south.

We both turned our heads,
Our bodies pursued.
We spun, we twirled—
We danced.

Time passed
Slowly,
Yet all too fast.
We smiled, we laughed,
Then suddenly passed.

Inertia was stronger
Than gravity's pull—
A well-traveled rut
That captures the wheel.

Neither one able
To alter their course,
Neither one willing
To give up their force.

And so we continued
On opposite paths,
Until the next time,
When we would collide.

LOVE PUNCH

He stopped as part of his routine,
While she just wanted some caffeine.
They both would leave with something more
Than either one was searching for.

It started with a ling'ring glance
That hinted at a greater chance,
But then she punched him in the chest
And instantly he lost his breath.

She met his gaze and bared her teeth
While standing safely out of reach.
Interpreting a challenge, he
Prepared for further injury.

Afraid he might antagonize
He quickly turns away his eyes,
Immediately searching for
The quickest pathway to the door.

No sign of interest perceived,
She thought that she would be relieved,
And yet her heart can't find a beat;
Her flesh is burned by inner heat.

Still reeling from initial shock
And deafened by the ticking clock,
He grabs his order, walks away,
Returning to a normal day.

He braves one last look over shoulder
Lamenting that he'd not been bolder.
But he's committed to his chore—
A duty he could not ignore.

There is an aching in the heart
Which lingers after they depart;
A wound that even time can't mend,
Nor any surgeon dare attend.

And while they never truly met,
The two of them will not forget
The words that neither one could say
That afternoon at the café.

FIELD DAYS

Beneath a cotton candy sky
Where we got low and we got high,
The air was filled with scent of beer,
The cries of joy, and screams of fear.

A night of laughter in the park;
A night of freedom in the dark.
Our shackles we had cast aside,
Bound only when we chose to ride.

Now free to try and free to fly;
Now free to live and free to die.
We chased each other round and round,
Between the lines of lost and found.

Hey, step right up and try your luck!
Get three more tries for just a buck!
Took careful aim but still a miss—
Without a prize, without a kiss.

Then guided by the flashing lights
And guarded by the passing frights,
We danced among the falling stars
To distant drums and steel guitars.

An impish twinkle in our eyes,
A crescent smile on the rise,
A memory on painted skin,
Where some things end and some begin.

CONSUMING PASSION

Passion's heat consumes the flesh,
Yet somehow calms the mind.
The soul is left both cleansed and fresh
As past is left behind.

TO SEE THE LIGHT OF DAY

Awaken, morning's lordly light
And chase away the dark of night;
Away from you all chill does creep.
I wish I had your love to keep.
If strength inside me I could find
I'd whisper words so true and kind.
No beauty on Earth can compare
To when I see you, setting there.
Alas, upon each night we part,
I feel that tugging at my heart.
If only I had been so bold,
My hidden passions you'd be told.
I wish I had not waited long,
For now the morning's light has gone.

YOUR BEAUTY LIES BEHIND YOUR EYES

Your beauty lies behind your eyes
And not in front of mine—
Within the creases of your smile
And humble self-denial.

I do not love you for your looks,
But for your choice in books.
The greatest virtues you possess
Can't hide behind a dress.

Your laughter I adore above
The flavor of your lips.
Although I must admit, I love
The curving of your hips.

The qualities that I admire
Are not the kind which may expire.
If hair and teeth were to depart,
No less would you possess my heart.

LOVE'S PUREST EXPRESSION

I used to think that love
Expressed through sacrifice,
And only gifts thereof
Were able to suffice.

I blame my catholic cross,
Reminding what He gave—
That only through His loss
Could anyone be saved.

But this was not the lesson
He wanted us to live,
For love's purest expression
Instead is to forgive.

LOVE IS GREATER

Not a hunger, not a thirst,
Not a force of nature.
It can grow and never burst,
Love is something greater.

In the vacuum love exists,
Child of Mars and Venus.
In the darkness it persists,
Love is in between us.

Love we have is love we gave,
We cannot contain it.
Ere the cradle, after grave,
We cannot explain it.

Love is love, and that's enough—
No need to define it.
For the soft and for the rough,
Even those who spite it.

GIVE AND TAKE

A LESSON REFUSED

My loving mother oft would scold,
"Not every glitter comes from gold."
Though many times have I been told,
I seek to have what I can't hold.

My father made it very plain,
"The chasing dog has naught to gain.
If you so seek to love in vain,
You shall return with naught but pain."

But I learn best from each mistake.
What scant advice I chose to take
Has kept my head above the lake,
Though soon I fear my will would break.

My legs have run in every race,
But never do I seem to place.
I wonder if in vain I chase,
And how long I can keep this pace.

What happens when my knees give out
And I have not the breath to shout?
Would still my heart be filled with doubt
If I had chose another route?

No longer can I wait my turn.
Too strongly my desires burn.
For the impossible I yearn—
One lesson I refuse to learn.

THE DREAMER

"Hey, Poppie! Poppie, look at me!
I have a magic boat!
It's free to ride, so come inside!
And watch it! Watch it float!"

"That's nice, my boy. Now take your toy
And hurry off to bed.
With Mother's song, where dreams belong,
God rest your little head.

"Then when you wake, make no mistake
In darkness, dreams will stay.
For dreams will fade as summer shade
Beneath the light of day.

"You'll learn that dreams are foolish lies
To comfort little boys;
When later you become a man,
You'll find no simple joys.

"Hard work and sweat to pay your debt—
The duty of a man.
You do not do what you want to,
You just do what you can.

"And then some day, when old and grey
You'll look back on your life
And sigh relief in disbelief,
Then lay down with your wife.

"You see, your play can't take away
The need to do your chores.
Through sun or rain, or health or pain,
They cannot be ignored.

"But when complete, naught can compete
With that accomplishment.
So now, my son, I pray you're done
With wasteful merriment.

"Be not confused, you're not abused
I do this for your good.
You must prepare and be aware,
As every young man should."

"But father why is it that I
Must toil till old age?
What's wrong with fun while work gets done?
Would that affect my wage?

"Is it so wrong to sing a song
While working in the yard?
Where comes this thought? When were you taught
That all that's good is hard?

"I disagree with your decree
That virtue's cost is pain.
Don't misconstrue, I still love you
So please let me explain.

"If I were you, and you were me,
I'd tell it differently.
I'd tell my son to go have fun,
For only dreams are free.

"I'd turn a chore to something more—
A game for us to play.
Then he'd desire to perspire,
Not to disobey."

CUTTER

With beer in his hand, and sun on his back,
I watched as that lad made a fearsome attack.
His blades whirling left, his blades whirling right,
He slices through every opponent in sight.

They tremble in fear, they shake at his might,
Unable to flee from their oncoming plight.
No hope of escape, they're rooted in place,
Accepting their fate with unmatchable grace.

He wipes away sweat that beads on his face
With fair maiden's token once bordered in lace
Now stained by the wars of present and past
And all the atrocities he has amassed.

Her symbol of love now naught but a rag.
It's dangling limply, a sad little flag.
And yet he returns upon noble steed
To answer her summons when she is in need.

He gives them no thought, he leaves them to
          bake,
Those legions of bodies he leaves in his wake.
And all who oppose, or dare to defy
Are broken if they do not bend and comply.

Returning to home, he washes his hands,
There's no grand parade, there's no marching
bands,
Just one weary man...
And one empty can...

BLOOD FOR BLOOD

Between his fingers, purple-black,
He held his hard-earned snack.
His pleasantly contented grin
Belied his broken skin.

For me it seemed too much to ask;
Too arduous a task.
I thought it far too small a gain
To justify the pain.

"How is it that you trust the fruit
From such a violent root?"
I ask him, standing in the mud.
"'Tis only blood for blood:

An even trade of flesh for flesh.
I should expect no less."
He paused to contemplate his prize,
A twinkle in his eyes.

"But if you seek a painless yield
Beware of what's concealed.
For those that want to take our lives
Use poison 'stead of knives."

SUNBATHER

Spreading her towel across the warm sand,
Book at her side and a drink in her hand.
Flips a few pages and takes a few sips,
Models the smile she'd drawn on her lips.

Skin baked to bronze underneath the clear skies.
Warm and contented she closes her eyes.
Soothed by the whispers of surf to the sand,
Lulled into sleep by the lack of demand.

While she is resting the sky fills with clouds.
Cut off from comfort by darkening shrouds,
Torn from her slumber by sharp, frigid breeze,
Eyes flashing louder than thundering seas.

Cool rain is falling so she runs inside,
Angry at having her pleasure denied.
Moments ago she'd been singing his praise,
Lavishing in his affectionate rays.

Cussing and cursing she spits on his name,
Piling upon him a mountain of blame.
Hates him for hiding behind that thick veil,
Hates that he travels upon a fixed rail.

Outraged at losing her comfortable spot,
Past is discarded, his presents forgot.
Packing her things up with outward disdain,
Numb to the drumming of sea-tainted rain.

"How could you do this!" she shouts at the sky,
Driving away without wondering why.
Finally, after the grey curtain clears,
He'll see that she left because of his tears.

I DON'T BRUISE

"Be gentle," I told her
"I've injured my shoulder"
As, slowly, I took off my shirt.

My stoic expression
Betrayed my confession—
She didn't believe I was hurt.

"I see no contusion."
She said with confusion
And more than a little disdain.

My mood it grew worse
Lamenting my curse
To suffer invisible pain.

PECKED OUT

The oak to the woodpecker:
   Dauntless provider.
So selflessly giving of
   All that's inside her.

Never complaining.
Never restraining.

Until she is hollowed
   And crashed to the ground.
And that selfish bird is
   Nowhere to be found.

ROTTEN

Something in my fridge is rotten.
Probably something long forgotten.
Long neglected and ignored,
Just used once and then got stored.

Buried in the dark and cold,
Getting old and growing mold.
Clearly I've held on too long,
Who could know it'd go so wrong?

Fooled by its duplicity:
Flavorful toxicity.
Stomach hurts, so I retire.
Ultimately, I expire.

DON'T GO TO BED WITH A DIRTY SINK

Don't sleep and leave a dirty sink
Don't let those dishes languish
Or else you'll wake to quite a stink
And break your fast with anguish

1 + 1 = 3

I gave myself to you,
You gave yourself to me.
Once one and one was two,
But now it equals three.

Through many sleepless nights,
And many hollow fights,
Remaining side-by-side,
A husband and his bride.

But then there came another
And nearly we're outnumbered.
Apart more than together,
Discussing only weather.

The universe maintains
A balance that sustains—
A delicate design
Whose pieces intertwine.

We've thrown off with our sum,
This equilibrium.
Now that we've multiplied
It seems we must divide.

A HUG GOES BOTH WAYS

Oh, hello my dear,
I'm so glad you're home!
It's been a hard day
For me all alone.

I know that you're tired.
I see that you're stressed.
I'll open the tap
While you get undressed.

Some candles will help
To settle your mood.
And while you relax,
I'll make up some food.

Then after you're done,
Come cuddle with me.
We'll have some dessert
And watch some TV.

But you say you need
Some time on your own,
And as you depart
I quietly groan.

Although it is hard
To handle rejection,
I'll swallow my pride
And save my affection.

You know that my love
Has no strings attached,
I know in your heart
My feelings are matched.

You say that you've had
"Just one of those days."
But lucky for me
A hug goes both ways.

STAINED

I realize to my surprise
How much paint brushes hide.
For all they put upon the wall,
There's more they keep inside.

When I observe its full reserve
Go flowing down the drain,
It feels a waste—like I've erased
A mem'ry from a brain.

When next I paint I see a taint
Of hue that I'd used last.
A thing begun can't be undone—
The future's stained by past.

A STIRRING OF COALS

The last to bed and first to rise,
Now questioning my open eyes.
I take a pause to acclimate
Before I try to navigate.

My bare feet on the frozen floor
Direct me toward my foremost chore.
Before a tomb of cold, black steel
I take my place and humbly kneel.

A silent prayer on trembling lips.
Cold iron numbs my fingertips.
I can't relax until rekindled
Which has, while in the darkness, dwindled.

With gentle motions I expose
A hidden cache of glowing coals.
The ember holds the soul of fire
Remaining after flames expire.

With care I place the eager tinder
Among the faintly glowing cinder.
And with a gentle, lover's breath
I call back life from throes of death.

Although I'm eager, I must wait—
Too much too quick will suffocate.
Then as the heat intensifies
I may add twigs of greater size.

The kindling sparks a greater blaze
Which burns my cheek and binds my gaze.
But this intensity can't last
For it consumes its fuel too fast.

Its purpose only preparation
To build a greater conflagration,
Without which I could not ignite
The logs to burn throughout the night.

The heat subsides but still remains,
A steady warmth which long sustains.
The temperature not cold or hot,
Its presence easily forgot.

A long, protracted consummation,
Just outside of observation;
A passion masked as obligation,
Smoldering in isolation.

A BURDEN SHARED

What was, from her, removed by force,
He yields without remorse.
He cannot stand to see her bear
A burden he could share.

And yet—despite his selflessness—
He cannot grant her this.
Her misery would not divide,
Instead it multiplied.

Their pain, it seems, will not accept
Lavoisier's precept.
No anguish can convert to joy,
Nor happiness destroy.

Throughout their struggles all they've known
Is how to be alone.
Until they choose a shared belief,
They will not find relief.

And so they make a leap of faith
Into each other's arms.
And in this desperate, last embrace
Reclaim forgotten charms.

DEMONS, QUESTS, AND PESTS

THE PASSENGER

I rode the train out to the end,
Got off and then got on again.
But now the train is going back
The way it came along the track.

I pass the stops I did not take
To find where I made my mistake.
Around me always something new,
An ever changing point of view.

The people come and then they go,
No time to stop and say hello.
They run to places I have passed
While sitting still, yet moving fast.

I do not understand the way
They go about their lives each day.
When there is so much they don't see,
How can they live so carelessly?

They fear of things they do not know
While running fast, yet moving slow.
Until they try to figure out
Those things that they have come to doubt,

And they go back the way they came
To see the world in different frame,
All by myself I shall remain
Among the faces on the train.

OPEN MIND

An open eye is often blind,
But never is an open mind.
Listen with more than the ear,
And more than ever will you hear.

MICE IN THE ATTIC

To the comfort and protection
Of my bedroom I retire
For a moment's introspection
Ere the rest that I require.

As I let the day's demands grip
Fade like echoes in the vale,
Grains of golden hourglass sands slip,
Draining from a pregnant pail.

From my burdens I'm retreating
'neath a heavy down embrace.
Cool kiss is my pillow's greeting
To my weary, burning face.

Closing heavy-lidded eyes and
Loosing grip of neck on head.
Long exhale my last command, then
Yielding body into bed.

Ere my dreams, an interfering,
Gentle but incessant itch
Scratches just inside my hearing,
Causing weary eyes to twitch.

With tightened lids and measured breath
I will for sleep to swift return.
Naught save the endless peace of death
Could grant to me that which I yearn.

The sounds that come from up above
Attempt to burrow through my brain.
I grasp my pillow and I shove
My head beneath to block the pain.

I can't avoid nor hope escape
Incessant and unending scrape.
I hear their small teeth gnawing,
Scratching, biting, digging, clawing.

Writhing 'neath a useless blanket.
Need to act, I cannot take it.
Something in that needs be out—
Stifling a primal shout.

I leap and punch the ceiling where
I hear the sound and hope to scare
These tiny creatures into stopping
All their scraping, chewing, popping.

I try and try to no avail.
Each plan appears destined to fail.
With fury borne of desperation,
Grown from simple agitation,

Well past peaceful resolution
And no hope of absolution,
I grab the witch's implement
And strike with venomous intent.

The ceiling hence is perforated;
Defenses I have penetrated.
I can see into their lair!
To kill them all, I gravely swear.

Yet still I hear them nipping,
And more tightly I am gripping.
The rage wells up within me
And I'm swinging violently.

Falling down upon my face,
Revealing only empty space.
Things that should have stayed unknown
Now to the light are shown.

In spite of my heroic feats,
The evidence upon my sheets,
Their fitful chewing yet resumes.
Their gnashing teeth, my thoughts consumed.

Digging at my spine.
Digging at my mind.
Why won't they just leave?
Are they that naive?

To clear this infestation
I would go to any end.
If I must I'll burn it down
And start it all again.

INK BLOT

I am an ink blot
On blank paper.
I began as an idea;
An action well-intentioned.
But the instant that the pen had struck,
I went in all directions.
Through the microscopic contours,
Connecting all the lines of fate.
One path leads me to the next,
I follow every fork,
I open every door.
What started as a point,
A fertile but unplanted seed,
Has grown and multiplied
Quite organically.
And what was meant to be a tree
Is now a patch of weeds.

MORE MICE IN THE ATTIC

The mice are in my attic.
I hear them every night.
As soon as it gets quiet,
They start to scratch and bite.

I waited for a minute
For them to take a rest.
Those bastards are persistent—
A clear and present pest.

'Twas clear I had no power
And so I plugged my ears.
But after half an hour
I'd almost gone to tears.

Skritching, scratching, nipping, gnawing—
Someone make it stop!
Biting, digging, chewing, clawing—
Head's about to pop!

Like a thousand tiny feet are
Scrambling up my spine.
Marching one after another
In an endless line.

I can feel my thoughts corroding,
Gnawing on my head.
I can feel my dreams eroding,
Slipping from my bed.

For a time I fed them poison...
Temporary fix.
Looking back, it seems the reason
I myself was sick...

There are mice in my attic.
I hear them every night.
As soon as it gets quiet,
They start to scratch and bite.

I'm not sure how they got there,
Or how to get them out.
I raise my fist into the air
And struggle not to shout.

With poison off the menu
I'm anxious for a way
To oust them from this venue
Before the end of day.

With glittering of madness
In red and sleepless eye
I conjure up a plan that's
At least as mad as I.

I find and block all entrances;
I will not let more in.
Alone I'll have to take my chances
With lingering vermin.

And yet they seem to multiply
Despite my firm blockade.
Regardless of how hard I try,
I cannot stop this raid.

It seems they've taken residence;
I've waited far too long.
And now I've set some precedents
Which cannot be withdrawn.

This home is what they're after—
I logically conclude—
I'll tear down every rafter
And throw out all the food.

Deprive them food and shelter—
The only way I'll win.
So I pick up my crowbar
And promptly I begin.

The plaster falling down like snow
Is like a winter dream.
And yet somehow I think I know,
Things are not what they seem.

The mice are in my attic.
I hear them every night.
As soon as it gets quiet,
They start to scratch and bite.

THE WELL

I took my gold out to the well
And threw it all inside.
Convinced, I was, its depths would be
The perfect place to hide.
But when I needed funds withdrawn,
The well returned me none.

CATCHING LIGHT

Out in a field on a warm summer night
Barehanded I captured a flickering light.
A single celestial plucked from the sky
By lonesome terrestrial wandering by.

A notion since childhood I'd been enchanted,
That by falling stars could our wishes be granted.
I felt electricity tickling my palm
And found it quite difficult to remain calm.

'Tween fingers I whispered my greatest desire
And silently waited for it to transpire.
But often when looking more closely at dreams
You'll find that the truth isn't quite what it seems.

And so as I open my hand to inspect,
I found that my wish had become an insect.

A MOMENTARY FLASH OF LIGHT

A momentary flash of light
Illuminates the dark of night.
A brilliant burst across the sky
Whose trailing sparkles slowly die.
A trembling boom that resonates
And viscerally penetrates.

No time to pause and ruminate,
The pace starts to accelerate
As more and more begin to fly
It's harder to identify
And isolate a single sight
With all the rockets taking flight.

A crackling cacophony
That synthesize a symphony
Which has a similar lament
For those who love one instrument
And pounds like drums upon the ears
To drown out the ensuing cheers.

And after the conclusion there
Continues a confusion where
An obfuscating cloud of mist
Around the people will persist.
The smell of brimstone in the air
Will clog the nose and cling to hair.

But etched upon the inner eye
Remain those visions from the sky.
The shape is absolutely true
Though lost, it has, its vibrant hue.
And still I find my way despite
A momentary flash of light.

THE ETERNAL BATTLE

The aging knight, his horse long passed,
Will don his armor for one last
Engagement with immortal foe—
A war that started long ago.

His joints crack as he leaves his bed
And straps his helmet to his head.
He struggles with his armor's buckles,
Fumbling with stiff, swollen knuckles.

He takes with him his shield and sword,
With which he served his former Lord.
Back when he stood both tall and proud,
Before his back was bent and bowed.

He stiffly shuffles down the street
With eyes diverted toward his feet
While passing hollow, lifeless shells
Where once there echoed playful yells.

The silent forest he traverses
Whispers ancient, evil curses,
Claws at him with bony fingers—
Icy touch long after lingers.

Arriving on the field at last
To face his rival from the past,
But feeling like a spineless fool
For honoring this senseless duel.

Between them countless battles fought,
Though each of them has been for naught,
For every time that they engage
Perpetuates the war they wage.

His foe is careful to conceal,
Behind a cloak of polished steel,
All trace of his identity
And so preserve their enmity.

While hate resides within his heart
The battle's lost before its start
And as their conflict stretches longer,
The enemy grows ever stronger.

Then suddenly the fight commences,
Before he's mustered his defenses.
His precedent won't let him yield
And so he ducks behind his shield.

Although he's spared a gruesome death,
The impact takes away his breath.
It leaves him lying on his back,
Preparing for the next attack.

One final strike to end his plight—
An end to their eternal fight.
But once again it doesn't come
And he is left, alone and numb.

JUST A TRICKLE

In earth a small depression,
Gathering the dew.
The tiniest impression,
Becoming something new.

Its contents slowly growing—
Gradually increased.
Until it's overflowing—
Forcibly released.

The hungry trickle gnawing
Gently at the mud.
A slow and steady sawing,
Channeling the flood.

The soil's emigration:
Imperceptible.
A secretive migration
Further down the hill.

As winter ice is thawing,
Flowing to the spring,
Its gravity is drawing—
Pressure deepening.

A hunger has awakened.
Swelling bud has bloomed.
And all that can be taken
Quickly is consumed.

Replacing earth with water
Til the water dries.
Upon a barren altar—
Sacrificial lies.

As grain for drop was traded,
Barriers dissolved.
A memory now faded
Self from self absolved.

The blood has worn the flesh and
Now reveals the bones.
In darkness tears are summoned,
Splashing on the stones.

A thirsty river flowing,
Never to be quenched.
Continually growing,
Solidly entrenched.

MUD MAN

Squishing and squirming my way through the mud
—

The way that I've been every day since the flood,
When pounding of waves ground the old
          mountains down
And Earth became covered in one shade of
          brown.

My foot strikes some earth that's more solid than
          soft
And trembling legs lift my body aloft.
How long it had been since I'd stood up erect
That I had forgotten just what to expect.

Slowly I rise up and out of the muck,
Pulling apart from the ground with a suck.
In horror I watch as my flesh is dissolving,
Yet knowing survival depends on evolving.

I panic and grab at a plummeting drip
Which oozes and seeps through my tightening
          grip.
Firm fingers of ice squeeze my chest and I gasp
As more of my body slips through my firm grasp.

The dripping slows down as I dry and I crack
And I know that soon there'll be no turning back,
For once I'm exposed there's no doubt that I'll
        burn
And so I relax, and to mud I return.

MIRED

A traveler stares in consternation.
'Tween him and his destination,
Veiled beneath a gossamer fog,
Hid a hungry bubbling bog.

'Cross the surface spirits danced.
Watching, he became entranced.
By compulsion, followed them
'Til the darkness swallowed him.

Close to where he could have crossed,
Turned away and quickly lost.
Can't go forward, can't go back,
Searching for a hidden track.

Stops to take a look around,
Slowly sinking in the ground.
Every moment that he thinks,
Deeper in the slime he sinks.

Has to choose but can't decide;
Once he does, he cannot stride.
Guided by his fear and panic,
Movements jerky and erratic.

Now exhausted and entombed,
He accepts that he is doomed.
As his mind and body numb
He refuses to succumb.

Desperately he tries to shout,
Letting in what had been out.
By the mud his words, suppressed,
Suffocate within his chest.

THE NEXT STEP

One foot in the sky
I step to eternity
The wind brings me back

SHE CAN FLY

They throw her side-eyed glances
And tell her she can't play.
She opts to take her chances,
Despite what they might say.
Stretching up and taking hold
She's never felt this bold.

One deep breath—first in, then out—
And then she makes her move.
Holding tight she wants to shout
But knows that she must prove
To all that undeniably
She is as strong as he.

Reaching out, hand over hand,
She slowly makes her way.
Her arms begin to tremble and
Her legs begin to sway.
She fears that she will lose her grip
As fingers start to slip.

Giving up is not a choice
So she holds on tighter
And tells the world without her voice
That she is a fighter.
When at last she'd reached the end,
She turned and went again.

Through her courage she has found
Her feet may leave the ground;
By daringly defying,
She is capable of flying.

FREE SPIRIT

A spirit free, yet Earthly caged
Is bound to dance along
A path that's all but prearranged,
Yet chooses she the song.

Her head wreathed by celestial fire,
Feet firmly on the ground.
Above her plays a holy choir
Of golden strands unbound.

Her steps strike true without a glance,
Her eyes fixed straight ahead.
And yet no things are left to chance—
She leads, or she is led.

CALMING STORM

I sleep the soundest in the rain,
Find solace in the storm.
The rhythmic drumming on the pane,
The blankets dry and warm.

I find if silence is too great,
I cannot concentrate;
There is no sound to override
The voices from inside.

So let the thunder rip and tear!
Let lightning scorch the sky!
While I stay safe within my lair,
Their battle outweighs mine.

When next I must go out-of-doors
The chilling rain yet pours.
I boldly stride into the fray,
One cannot sheltered stay.

Against the wind I must resist.
The rain yet gives me cause.
A fight through which I must persist,
Advancing without pause.

But when the sun is shining bright,
And nothing's left to fight,
I have no cause to persevere,
And so, I disappear.

LURKING DEMONS

In the darkness, demons lurk
Down beneath the muck and murk.
Feasting off the death and rot
While they multiply and plot.
Hidden from our mortal eyes—
Hidden by our mortal lies.

Faces, by the shadows blurred,
Stalk the unsuspecting herd.
Blowing a beguiling breeze,
Spreading famine and disease.
Shepherds pay the signs no heed,
Blinded by hubris and greed.

Silently the plague is spread,
Suddenly the flock is dead.
Having honed their deadly skills,
Hungry now for greater kills,
Roaming farther from their lair,
Cloaked in shadow and despair.

Cultivating the unknown,
From which, doubt and fear are grown.
Anger wields a razor scythe,
Reaping an expensive tithe.
Once collected, not replaced—
Sovereignty has been effaced.

By the darkness, truth concealed.
Weakness by the light revealed.
Virtue melts their strength away—
Shadows can't survive the day.
The night is dark and ages long,
But always broken by the dawn.

BLACK AND BLUE

You hit me and I hit you,
All we see is black and blue.
Wearing wounds in open view,
Signaling the retinue.

Everything is black and white.
Only way to win's to fight.
Sharply swinging left and right,
Spurred along by fear and spite.

Bringing others to our side,
Equal parts belief and pride,
Heeding only those allied—
Voices inward amplified.

Onward trading eye for eye,
All the while we wonder why
Others seem forever blind,
Stunted by a calloused mind.

Darkness and Light

Is white on black, or black on white?
Can there be darkness without light?
And what is day without the night?

One cannot see when it's too bright
And darkness also robs one's sight.
A balance there must always be,
Else no one in the world can see.

DROWN THEM OUT

The demons whispering in my ear
Fill mind with lies and heart with fear.
And so I tried to drown them out,
At first with wine and then with beer.

Their potency I start to doubt,
When every whisper turns to shout.
I seek a method to enshroud
These trespassers I cannot rout.

Their voices I have disallowed;
Their presence I have disavowed.
And I have made my thinking clear
By turning up the music loud.

INVOKING THE SPIRITS

My soul, it was restrained;
In heavy irons, chained.
Impossible to break,
My hope was my mistake.

Through ancient ritual,
Invoked the spiritual.
Thus freed by spectral force,
My instincts ran their course.

Now uninhibited,
With naught prohibited.
No recourse or regret.
No mem'ries to forget.

Unguided by my nerves,
I cashed in my reserves.
'Til all my spending spent;
'Til sleepy and content.

I lay and closed my eyes,
But woke to foul surprise:
Those spirits from the night
Would burn in holy light.

They promised absolution.
Their gift was an illusion.
I'd thought my wishes granted,
But they had been supplanted.

Released from my containment
For fiendish entertainment.
Their appetites now sated
They left me, lone and naked.

HUNGOVER

Woke up wearing all my clothes.
How I got here; no one knows.
Went to bed while feeling happy,
Woke up feeling pretty crappy.

Mouth is dry and head is aching—
Ibuprofen I'll be taking.
Time for me to rehydrate,
Pray to God I won't be late.

Piece together what transpired
And, with luck, I won't get fired.
What the devil was I thinking?
That's the last time I go drinking!

HOW TO FIGHT DEMONS

The thing about demons that many don't know:
The harder you fight them, the stronger they
        grow.
An overly cunning and devious foe,
To beat one requires the strength to let go.

TO SLEEP, TO DREAM, TO WRITE

TO NIGHT

To bed to rest my weary head,
Where dreams and fantasy are wed.
To close my eyes and see the sights
That can't be seen beneath the lights.

To wake refreshed with autumn's dawn,
My first breath crisp and deeply drawn.
To toil through the working day
And then return to home to play.

To play until the playing ends
And rest again, among my friends.

TOMORROW IS COMING

Tomorrow is a mystery,
Today is ancient history.
The future is the past,
The present cannot last.
Dangerous to wait.
Do not hesitate.
To them be true,
Say "I love you"
Before
It is—

DREAM JUICE

If I lay down and tip my head,
My thoughts will spill across my bed.
And then I'll have to mop them up,
And wring them out into a cup.
I'll add some vodka and some ice,
Then mix it once and shake it twice.
I'll drink it with a dash of cream
And wait as thoughts blend to a dream.

RESTLESS

Eyeballs are burning,
Kitten is purring,
Time to lie down in my bed.

Tossing and turning,
Spinning and stirring,
Thoughts won't lie down in my head.

Pining and yearning,
A theme reoccurring,
Tugging on every loose thread.

Hours of churning,
Soundlessly whirring,
Reading again what was read.

FLOWING

Feet tappin', head boppin'
Fingers twitchin', they ain't stoppin'
Unimpeded soul translation
Empty minded recitation
Emotions flowing to the page
Boundless love to seething rage
Imagination running wild
Reality has been exiled
Finally free from all oppression
Indulging in my mind's obsession
Living out a fantasy
In an absentee reality
Carried by the cadency
Of a rousing melody

FLOP

In my head it's buzzing,
But on my tongue it stops.
It twists and flips and falters,
And on the floor it flops.

Choking, gasping, wanting air—
It's not long for this world.
A fish that's out of water
With no hope of return.

A once majestic creature,
Graceful as can be,
But only in its element
Where no one else can see.